English --- Telugu
Conversation guide

Aarthi Janyavula

Copyright © 2018 by Aarthi Janyavula
All rights reserved

First printing, May 2018

ISBN 9781983021312

Illustrations by Fano and AC

Contents

Foreword 9

Chapter 1: Essentials 12

Chapter 2: Greetings/Introducing yourself 36

Chapter 3: Languages 40

Chapter 4: Travel and transports 44

Chapter 5: Shopping 54

Chapter 6: Eating and drinking 60

Chapter 7: Entertainment 74

Chapter 8: Help and emergency 80

Chapter 9: Body 84

Chapter 10: Health and hospital 88

Chapter 11: Time 92

Chapter 12: Family and relationships 98

Chapter 13: On the phone 104

Chapter 14: Emotions and feelings 108

Chapter 15: Animals 112

Chapter 16: Weather 116

Chapter 17: Sports 120

Chapter 18: Signals 124

Chapter 19: Authority 126

Chapter 20: At work 130

Chapter 21: At home 134
Chapter 22: Colors 138
Appendix 142
Appendix B 143
Appendix C 145
Appendix D 152

Foreword

Learning a language requires patience, strong will to learn and a lot of practice. We made our best effort in trying to make this journey of yours easier. This book doesn't explain much about Telugu grammar but it will certainly show you a quick road to learn some frequently used words, memorise them and thereby use them in framing your own sentences. The learning path should still include a bit of grammar, that we included in the form of tips and tricks at different places of the book.

The book's **focus is mainly on colloquial Telugu** as we intend to keep it more useful for people who come for a short visit to Telugu speaking states in India and have a quick guide in how to converse. Remember that, colloquial Telugu that most of the people speak is a mix of English and Telugu (sometimes Hindi as well in places like Hyderabad but it's minimal). For example, if you want to say *Thank you* in Telugu, we don't use *Kruthagnathalu* or *Dhanyavadalu* in conversations. We just say *Thank you* or *Thanks*. In order to understand what kind of Telugu translation we have provided, we added below tags for words/sentences:

- **Traditional** - to represent words/sentences in authentic Telugu which might not be used in daily life by everyone except by very few people.
- **Colloquial** - to represent words/sentences used in daily life by most of the people.

- **Casual** - to represent words/sentences to use with people younger than you or with people of same age as you.
- **Formal** - to represent words/sentences to use with elder people, people we do not know or to whom we owe respect.

Traditional words will give you some idea if by any chance if the opposite person is speaking pure Telugu, and you will at least understand what they are saying to keep you in a comfortable situation and be able to respond back.

We provided some analogies/correlations with other languages as well like Hindi/French/English to understand Telugu better. We believe that it is easier to remember words by correlations with your own languages rather than learning something from scratch.

Tip: Read the tips carefully as it will help you in making your own sentences at later point of time.

Sometimes you see "..." in between sentences. This is a word to fill in during your translation from English to Telugu. For example,
   Can you call ...
   ... ni pilavandi
Here, ... is the name of the person or any other subject the sentence is referring to.

We advice you to focus more on first chapter and move to other chapters once you master it. It will help you to understand others chapters more easily.

We made our best effort to make this book easy to understand. Please leave your feedback or suggestions to us at
english.telugu.guide@gmail.com

Chapter 1: Essentials

Yes
Avunu

No
Kaadu

No/Don't have
Ledhu

Ok (as an acknowledgment)
Sare

Ok (as an agreement)
Alage

Don't know
Raadhu/Telidu

Thank you
Thank you, Thanks (colloquial)
Kruthagnathalu/Dhanyavadalu (traditional)

No, thank you
Akkarledhu
Parvaledhu

Please
Dayachesi

Excuse me / Sorry
Sorry (casual)
Kshaminchandi (formal)

Maybe
Bahusa

Come in/Come
Randi (formal)
Raa (casual)

Tip: *Telugu verbs have two forms. A formal form, to use with elders and a casual form to use with younger or people of same age. To make a formal form of a verb, replace last letter in the verb with andi. For example, 'Raa + andi = Randi'. This works for most of the cases except a few exceptions that we will discuss later. Congratulations!!!! You just learnt your first word joining in Telugu.*

Take
Tisuko (casual)
Tisukondi (formal)

I forgot
Marchipoyanu

It does not matter / It is ok
Parvaledhu

One moment please/One minute please
Okka nimisham

Really?
Nijamga?

It is very important
Idi chala mukhyam

I am coming now
Nenu ippudu vasthunnanu

I will be back in a few minutes
Nenu konni nimushallo tirigi vasthanu

And you?
Mari meeru?

Isn't it?
Kaada?

Anything else?
Inkenti? (inka + enti)

Are you sure?
Meeru cheppedi nijama? (formal)
Nuvvu cheppedi nijama? (casual)

I know
Naaku telusu

I do not know
Naaku telidu

I understand
Naaku ardham ayindhi

I do not understand
Naaku ardham kaledhu

No idea
Telidu

Pronouns

I
Nenu

Me
Nannu

You
Nuvvu (singular casual)
Meeru (singular formal)
Meeru (plural)

Tip: *We use the same word (Meeru) for plural form and also for formal form of the 'You'. For example, when you are speaking with an elder person, you should use 'meeru' (formal pronoun for elders) and you can use this word when you are speaking with group of children as well (as a plural form). But while speaking with one child in particular, you should use 'nuvvu' (as a singular casual word).*

He/Him
Athanu/Athadu (casual)
Aayana (formal)

She/Her
Aame (casual)
Aavida (formal)

We
Memu

They/Them
Vaaru/Vaallu

My
Naa

Your
Nee (singular casual)
Mee (singular formal/plural)

Mine
Naadi

His
Athani

Her
Aame

Our
Mana

Their
Vaalla (colloquial)
Vaari (traditional)

Tip: Sometimes in Telugu, we can make sentences to give quick and short replies. Above 3 are such words which can be used for single word sentences to say that "... (something) belongs to him/his/mine)". Below is an example conversation:
Person1: Whose book is this?
Person2: Athanidi (his book)/Aamedi (her book)
In the reply from the person2, the person just used word 'Athanidi/Aamedi' to express that 'book belongs to him/her' by using a single word. This is just one example using book, but it can be applied to any object.

This/It
Idi

That/It
Adi

These
Ivi

Those
Avi

Tip: *If you observe last 4 words, they are the same as their opposite forms except for first letter. This is similar to some other languages like Hindi (like words yaha/vaha, idhar/udhar). Words starting with 'I' are used to describe things near to you and 'A' for the words to describe the things far from you. You just need to change first letter to make it opposite form.*

Fact: Telugu is gender neutral language unlike other languages like Hindi/French. It is more similar to English where objects (things) do not have any gender (are gender neutral). Telugu might then be a bit easier for learning as you do not need to memorize genders of the things also along with vocabulary. For example, in French, a car is feminine but a truck is masculine. It exists in Hindi as well like, a chair is feminine but a bed is masculine. That's not the case with Telugu. Telugu is like English, car/truck/bicycle/chair/bed are objects without gender. Animals and birds are also gender neutral in Telugu. We will give some examples for this in subsequent chapters.

Questions

What
Enti

Who
Evaru

Why
Enduku

Why not
Endhuku kaadhu

How
Ela

Where
Ekkada

When
Eppudu

Which
Edi

How much
Entha

How many
Enni

Fact: All the questioning words in Telugu starts with 'E' just like the way they start with 'W' in English.

Fun Fact: And most of the time, you can make a response by just changing first letter of E to I/A. like response for Eppudu could be Appudu/Ippudu, or response for Edi could be Adi/Idi.

Numbers

0 - Sunna
1 - Okati
2 - Rendu
3 - Muudu
4 - Naalugu
5 - Aidhu
6 - Aaru
7 - Edu
8 - Enimidi
9 - Thommidi
10 - Padi
11 - Padakondu
12 - Pannendu
13 - Padamuudu (padi(10) + muudu(3))
14 - Padnalugu (padi(10) + naalugu(4))
15 - Padihenu
16 - Padahaaru (padi(10) + aaru(6))
17 - Padihedu (padi(10) + edu(7))
18 - Paddhenimidi (padi(10) + enimidi(8))
19 - Panthommidi (padi(10) + thommidi(9))
20 – Iravai

Note: After 20, it is easier to remember numbers because it is a direct concatenation of words. for instance, 21 is 'iravai okati' (iravai + okati), 22 is 'iravai rendu' (iravai + rendu)

30 - Muppai
40 - Nalabhai
50 - Yaabhai
60 - Aravai
70 - Debbai
80 - Enabhai
90 - Thombhai
100 - Vanda
1,000 - Veyyi
10,000 - Padi velu

Note: *Indian numbering system a bit different. As from 100,000. Please note the position of the coma/separator.*

1,00,000 (100,000) - laksha
10,00,000 (1,000,000) - padi lakshalu
1,00,00,000 (10,000,000) - Koti
10,00,00,000 (100,000,000) - padi kotlu
100,00,00,000 (1,000,000,000) - vanda kotlu
1000,00,00,000 (10,000,000,000) - veyyi kotlu
10000,00,00,000 (100,000,000,000) - padivela kotlu
100000,00,00,000 (1,000,000,000,000) - laksha kotlu
1000000,00,00,000 (10,000,000,000,000) - padi lakshala kotlu

Interesting fact: *Ancient astronomers in India calculated distance between many astronomical objects very precisely before telescope was even invented. Ancient mathematics is very well advanced to achieve these tasks for which they have invented words for some of the largest numbers than humanity can ever imagine for that time. Please refer to Appendix B for the names of those numbers They are originated in sanskrit and translated in Telugu.*

First
Modati
Second
Rendava
Third
Muudava

Tip: Replace last letter of number with 'ava' to get the position you want to say. For example:
Third = muudu + ava = muudava
Fourth = naalugu + ava = naalugava
First = okati + ava = okatava / modhati

Quantities

A lot / Much
Chala

Some/A bit/A little/few
Konni (countable)
Koncham (uncountable)

More
Ekkuva

Less
Thakkuva

Half
Ara

Full
Mothamu

Quarter
Paavu

Enough
Chaalu

Adjectives

Small
Chinna

Big
Pedha

Short (in terms of length)
Potti

Long (in terms of length)
Podugu

Beautiful
Andamaina

Ugly
Vikruthamaina

Thin
Sanna

Fat
Laavu

High
Etthu

Low
Pallam

Deep
Lothu

Heavy
Baruvu

Light (in weight)
Telika

Highest
Ethaina

Deepest
Lothaina

Note: The plural form of any noun is constructed by adding the "lu" suffix to the noun. Also, do not forget to change verb form to plural form along with your noun. You will find more about this in "Sentence building".

Prepositions/Conjunctions

For
Kosam (colloquial)
Koraku (traditional)

To
Ku

But
Kani

Because
Endukante

Because of
Valla

With
Tho

Without
Lekunda

From
Nundi/Nunchi

Till
Varaku

By
Dwara

After/Next
Tharuvatha

Before/Front
Mundu

Back
Venuka

Up
Paina

Down
Kinda

Between
Madhya

Except
Thappa

Out/Outside
Bayata

Inside
Lopala

In
Lo

Tip: In Telugu, sometimes we use 'in' (lo) instead of by (dwara). for example, to say "I came by bus", Telugu translation is "Bus lo vachanu", not "bus dwara vachanu".

Like
La/Laga

About
Gurinchi

And
Mariyu

Or
Leka/Leda

So
Kabatti

Main verbs

Ask
Adugu

Build
Nirminchu

Call
Piluvu

Catch
Pattuko

Come
Raa

Cook
Vandu

Drink
Thaagu

Eat
Thinu

Fly
Eguru

Give
Ivvu

Go
Vellu

Jump
Duuku

Laugh
Navvu

Look
Chudu

Open
Teruvu

Close
Musi

Make/Do
Cheyu

Swim
Eedu

Stop
Aapu

Sleep
Paduko

Read
Chauvu

Write
Raayu

Walk
Naduvu

Run
Parigethu

Say/Tell
Cheppu

Drive
Nadupu

Watch/See
Chudu

Listen/Hear
Vinu

Dance
Dance (colloquial)
Nruthyam (traditional)

Sing
Paadu

Study
Chaduvu

Clean
Shubram cheyu
Kadugu

Take
Tisukonu

Cut
Kathirinchu ... (a paper/cloth)
Koyyu ... (vegetables/cake)

Speak/Talk
Matladu

Think
Alochinchu

Look
Chudu

Use
Upayoginchu

Find
Vethuku

Walk
Nadupu

Try
Prayathninchu

Begin/Start
Prarambhinchu

Help
Sahaayam cheyu

Play
Aadu

Move
Kadulu

Note: These are just basic verbs to keep you making conversations in your daily life. Once you memorize these verbs, you just need to add a tense which is nothing but a suffix to the verb and person (first person/second person/third person) to construct your own sentences. And in most of the times the same suffices work for any verb.

Sentence construction

Below are the verb suffices for different forms in Telugu in present tense. Examples are based on verb vacha:

	Formal Singular	Casual Singular	Formal Plural	Casual Plural
First person (Male)	**nu** vachanu	**nu** vachanu	**mu** vachamu	**mu** vachamu
First person (Female)	**nu** vachanu	**nu** vachanu	**mu** vachamu	**mu** vachamu
Second person (Male)	**ru** vacharu	**vu** vachavu	**mu** vachamu	**mu** vachamu
Second person	**ru** vacharu	**vu** vachavu	**ru** vacharu	**ru** vacharu

(Female)				
Third person (Male)	**ru** vacharu	**du** vachadu	**ru** vacharu	**ru** vacharu
Third person (Female)	**ru** vacharu	**di** vachindi	**ru** vacharu	**ru** vacharu
Neutral gender	**di** vachindi	**di** vachindi	**yi** vachayi	**yi** vachayi

You can follow the rules above and apply it to any verb to conjugate it easily.

Let's start making sentences for verb *paduko* (sleep) including other tenses.

Past tense:
First person:
I Slept
Nenu paduk**unnanu**

We slept
Memu paduk**unnamu**

Second person:
You slept
Nuvvu paduk**unnavu**
Meeru paduk**unnaru**

Third person:
He slept
Athanu paduk**unnadu**(paduk**unnaru**)

She slept
Aame paduk**undhi**

It slept
Adi paduk**undhi**

Present tense:
First person:
I am sleeping
Nenu paduk**untunnanu**

We are sleeping
Memu paduk**untunnamu**

Second person:
You are sleeping
Nuvvu paduk**untunnavu**
Meeru paduk**untunnaru**

Third person:
He is sleeping
Athanu paduk**untunnadu**(paduk**unnaru**)

She slept
Aame paduk**untundhi**

It slept
Adi paduk**untundhi**

Future tense:
First person:
I will sleep
Nenu paduk**untanu**

We will sleep
Memu paduk**untamu**

Second person:
You will sleep
Nuvvu paduk**untavu**
Meeru paduk**untaru**

Third person:
He will sleep
Athanu paduk**untadu**(paduk**untaru**)

She will sleep
Aame paduk**untadi**

It will sleep
Adi paduk**untadi**

Few more sentences based on this verb:
I can sleep
Nenu paduk**ogalanu**

I should sleep
Nenu paduk**ovali**

I must sleep
Nenu **thappakunda** paduk**ovali**

Note: Just by memorizing the verbs and which suffix to add, you can make any kind of sentence in Telugu.

Chapter 2: Greetings/Introducing yourself

Hello
Namaskaram
Namasthe (Hindi word, but can be used in Telugu too)

Goodbye
Vellosthanu

Good morning
Shubhodayam

Good afternoon
Shuba dhinam

Good evening
Shuba saayantram

Good night
Shubha rathri

See you later
Malli kaludham

Nice to meet you
Mimmalni kalisinanduku santhosham

How are you?
Ela unnav? (casual)
Ela unnaru? (formal)

I am fine
Nenu bagunnanu

Congratulations
Abhinandanalu

Happy birthday
Puttinaroju Subhakankshalu
Janmadina Subhakankshalu

Happy new year
Nuuthana samvathsara subhakankshalu

Sir/Mr
Sri

Miss
Kumari

Mrs
Srimathi

What is your name?
Nee perenti? (casual)
Mee perenti? (formal)

My name is ...
Naa peru ...

Where are you from?
Nuvvu ekkada nunchi vachavu? (casual)
Meeru ekkada nunchi vacharu? (formal)

I am from India
Nenu India nunchi vachaanu

How old are you?
Nee vayasentha? (casual)
Mee vayasentha? (formal)

I am 25 years old
Naa vayasu 25

Who is he?
Evarathanu (Evaru + Athanu)

Who is she?
Evarame (Evaru + Aame)

Note: Some Telugu words can be combined into a single word like above. It is not so important for now, but if you want to learn more about word joining rules, please refer to appendix C. This is just to speak like local but there is nothing wrong even when you do not join the words.

Tell me
Cheppu (casual)
Cheppandi (formal)

What do you need?
Em kavali

Chapter 3: Languages

Language
Bhaasha

I speak English
Nenu English maatladathanu (colloquial)
Nenu aanglamu maatladathanu (traditional)

I speak a little Telugu
Nenu konchem Telugu maatladthanu

I do not speak Telugu
Nenu Telugu maatlaadanu

Do you speak english?
Nuvvu English maatladathaava? (casual)
Meeru English maatladathaara? (formal)

How many languages do you speak?
Nuvvu enni bhaashalu matladathavu? (casual)
Meeru enni bhaashalu matladagalaru? (formal)

You speak Telugu very well
Nuvvu Telugu chaala baaga maatladuthunnavu (casual)
Meeru Telugu chaala baaga maatladuthunnaru (formal)

I am learning Telugu
Nenu Telugu nerchukuntunnanu

How do you say... in Telugu?
... ni Telugu lo emantaru (emi + antaru)?

What is this?
Idi enti?

This is called...
Deenini ... antaru

What does it mean?
Idhi ante enti?

Could you repeat please?
Dayachesi malli okasari ... (... - whatever action to be repeated)
Dayachesi malli okasari chepthara (please, tell me again)

Could you speak slower please?
Dayachesi nemmadiga* matladagalara
Dayachesi nemmadiga* matladathara

Can you write it down?
Deenini Raayagalara?

How do you pronounce that?
Deenini ela palukuthaaru?

Can you translate this for me?
Deenini Naa kosam anuvadisthara?

Did you understand?
Meeku ardhamainda?

I understood
Naaku ardhamaindi

I did not understand
Naaku ardham kaaledhu?

Chapter 4: Travel and transports

Country
Desham

State
Rashtram

Region
Pradesham

Let's go!
Padha podham (casual)
Padhandi podham (formal)

I lost my luggage
Naa saamanu poindi (colloquial)
Nenu naa saamanu kolpoyanu (traditional)

When did you arrive?
Nuvvu eppudu cherukunnavu? (casual)
Meeru eppudu cherukunnaru? (formal)

Do you like India?
Neeku India nachinda? (casual)
Meeku India nachinda? (formal)

India is a very beautiful country
India chaala andamaina desham

I haven't been there yet
Nenu inka akkada ki vellaledhu

How was your trip?
Nee trip ela aindi? (casual)
Mee trip ela aindi? (formal)
Mee prayanam ela aindi? (traditional)

I want to go home
Naaku inti ki vellalani undhi

A ticket to Vizag
Vizag ki oka ticket

Locations

Here
Ikkada

There
Akkada

Everywhere
Anni chotla

Nearby
Parisarallo/daggara lo

Where are you?
Ekkada unnavu? (casual)
Ekkada unnaru? (formal)

Looking for a place

Destination
Gamyam

I would like to go to...
Naaku ... vellalani undhi

How can I go to...?
Nenu ... ki ela vellagalanu

Can you show me on the map?
Map lo chupinchagalara? (colloquial)
Patam lo chupinchagalara? (traditional)

I am looking for...
Nenu ... kosam chusthunnanu

Is it far?
Adi duuarama?

It is close
Adi daggara

Where is the city center?
City center ekkada?

Where are the toilets?
Toilets ekkada (colloquial)
Marugudhodlu ekkada (traditional)

What is the address
Address enti? (colloquial)
Chirunaama enti? (traditional)

How far is it?
Adi entha duuram?

It is not far
Adi duuram kaadu
Adi daggara (It is nearby)

I am lost
Nenu thappipoyanu

Follow me
Nannu anusarinchandi

Directions

(Next) Left/Right
(Tarvatha) Edama/Kudi

Turn left/right
Edama/Kudi vaipu tiragandi
Edama/Kudi vaipu tirugu

Straight ahead
Saraasari

Towards the...
... vaipu

Pass the...
... daatandi

North
Utharam

South
Dakshinam

East
Thuurpu

West
Padamara

That way
Atu vaipu

This way
Itu vaipu

In the car

Vehicle
Vaahanam

I want to rent a car
Naaku oka car adheku kavali

Note: There are no Telugu words for most of the vehicle names like car/motorbike/bus. These can be categorized as vaahanam (vaahanalu - plural). You can use the English words for all vehicles.

Can I park here?
Nenu ikkada park cheyagalana? (colloquial)
Nenu ikkada nilupagalana? (traditional)

Where is the nearest petrol/diesel station?
Daggara lo edaina petrol station unda?

The tire of my car is punctured
Naa car tire puncture aindi (colloquial)

There is a traffic jam
Vaahanalu nilichipoyayi (*Vehicles stopped* - There is no literal translation)

Other transports

Bus
Bus

Plane
Vimaanam

Taxi
Taxi

Can you call a taxi?
Taxi ni pilavagalara?

Take me to... please
Dayachesi ... ki tisukellagalara?

Train
Train (colloquial)
Railu bandi (traditional but not too old word)
Dhuumasakatam (traditional but too old word)

When does the train leave?
Train eppudu bayaluderuthundhi?

Where is the train to?
Train ekkada ki velthundhi?

Does the train stop in...?
Train ... lo aaguthunda?

When will the train arrive?
Train eppudu cheruthundhi?

Important places

Airport
Airport (colloquial)
Vimaanasrayam (traditional)

Train station
Railway station (colloquial)
Railway nilayam (traditional)

Bus station
Bus station

Hospital
Hospital (colloquial)
Aasupathri (traditonal)

Bank
Bank

ATM
ATM

Grocery store
Sarukula kottu
Kirana kottu

Pharmacy
Mandhula shop (colloquial)
Aushadha shaala (traditional)

Doctor
Doctor (colloquial)
Vaidhyudu (traditional)

Accommodation
Hotel
Hotel (colloquial)
Vididhi illu/gruham (traditional)

Hostel
Hostel (colloquial)
Vasathi gruham (traditional)

I have a reservation
Naaku reservation undhi

I would like to book a room for two people
Naaku idhariki saripada oka gadi ivvagalara

Do you have a room available?
Mee daggara oka gadhi unda?

How many nights do you want to stay?
Meeru enni rathrulu untaru?

How much is a room for one person?
Oka gadhi oka manishi ki entha?

How much is a room for two people?
Oka gadhi idhariki entha?

I will stay for one night
Nenu oka raathri untanu

Your reservation is confirmed
Mee reservation confirm aindi

When will the room be ready?
Room eppudu thayaravuthundhi?

What time is the checkout?
Checkout eppudu?

Did you enjoy your stay?
Meeku mee basa nachinda?

Is there a hair dryer in the room?
Room lo hairdryer untunda?

Is there a telephone in the room?
Room lo phone kuda untunda?

Is there a bathroom in the room?
Room lo bathroom untunda?

I need more pillows
Naaku inka konni dhindlu kavali

I need more towels
Naaku inka konni towels kavali (colloquial)
Naaku inka konni thuvallu kavali (traditional)

I need an additional quilt
Naaku inkoka raggu kuda kavali

The room is too cold
Gadhi chala challaga undhi

The room is too hot
Gadhi chala vedi ga undhi

Chapter 5: Shopping

Money

Rupee(s)
Rupaya(lu)

Tip: Adding lu to a word makes it plural.

Do you accept dollars?
Dollars tiskuntara?

How much is this?
Deeni kharidu entha?

Where is the nearest ATM?
Daggara lo ATM ekkada undhi?

Where is the nearest bank?
Daggara lo bank ekkada undhi?

I would like to transfer money
Nenu money transfer cheyyali

My bank account number is ...
Na bank account number ...

Can I pay by card?
Nanu card tho kattagalana?

We only accept cash
Memu dabbulu matrame tiskuntamu

Where can I get money changed?
Daggara lo foreign exchange ekkada?

What is the exchange rate?
Exchange rate entha?

I would like to exchange dollars against rupees
Nenu dollar nunchi rupees ki exchange cheyyali

Shop

Shop
Shop (colloquial)
Kottu (current)
Dukaanam (traditional)

When do you open?
Meeru eppudu terustharu?

When do you close?
Meeru eppudu muusivestharu?

How much is this?
Idi entha?

It is too expensive
Idi chaala kharidainadi

It is cheap
Idi chavaka

Do you have...?
Mee/Nee daggara ... unda?

Do you have a bag?
Mee daggara sanchi undha?

Can I try this on?
Idi nenu try cheyocha?

Do you have in another color?
Me daggara inkoka rangu unda?

I like this
Idi naaku nachindi

I do not like it
Idi naaku nachaledhu

It is too big
Idi chaala pedhadi

It is too small
Idi chaala chinnadi

I take size 40
Nenu 40 size tiskuntanu

Which one is better?
Edi better (colloquial)
Edi manchidi (traditional)

I am not interested
Interest ledhu (colloquial)
Aasakthi ledhu (traditional)

I will take one
Nenu okati tiskuntanu

I haven't decided
Nenu inka decide avvaledhu (colloquial)
Nenu inka nirnayinchukoledhu (traditional)

That is all, thank you
Anthe. Dhanyavadhalu

I would like to return this
Nenu idi tirigi ichi vedham anukuntunna

This is broken
Idi virigipoindi/pagilipoindi

This is for you
Idi nee/mee kosam

Chapter 6: Eating and drinking

Breakfast
Tiffin (colloquial)

Lunch
Bhojanam (meal - no literal Telugu word exists in Telugu for lunch and dinner)

Dinner
Bhojanam (meal - no literal Telugu word exists in Telugu for lunch and dinner)

Are you hungry?
Meeku aakaliga undha?

I am hungry
Naaku aakaliga undhi

I am not hungry
Naaku aakaliga ledhu

Are you thirsty?
Meeku daaham ga unda?

I am thirsty
Naaku daaham ga undhi

I am not thirsty
Naaku daaham ga ledhu

Did you have lunch?
Meeru bhojanam chesaara?

Would you like something to eat?
Meeku edaina tinalani unda?

My stomach is full
Naa kadupu nindindhi

I had enough
Naaku saripoindi

I will eat some more
Nenu inka tintanu

I can eat some more
Nenu inka tinagalanu

I must eat more
Nenu inka tinali
Nenu thappaka inka tinali (if you want to put more intensity on must)

I am a vegetarian
Nenu vegetarian (colloquial)
Nenu shaakahari ni (traditional)

Spoon
Spoon (colloquial)
Chemcha (traditional)

Fork
Fork (colloquial)
Palla chemcha (traditional)

Knife
Kathi/Chaaku

Spatula
Atlakaada

Foodstuffs

Meat
Mamsam

Chicken
Kodi mamsam

Lamb/Mutton
Gorre mamsam

Pork
Pandhi mamsam

Beef
Goddu mamsam

Fish
Chepa

Egg
Guddu/Gudlu

Bread
Bread (colloquial)
Rotte (traditional)

Noodles
Noodles

Rice
Biyyam (uncooked rice)
Annam (cooked rice)

Butter
Venna

Cream
Meegada

Sugar
Panchadhaara

Oil
Noone

Yoghurt
Perugu

Flour
Pindi

Tip: *All kinds of flour and batter are called as pindi in Telugu.*

Dal
Kandi pappu

Green gram
Pesara pappu

Black gram
Minapa pappu

Cake
Cake

Spices and herbs

Salt
Uppu

Pepper
Miriyaalu

Bay leaves
Biryani aaku

Cardamom
Yalakullu

Chilli powder
Kaaram

Cinnamon
Dalchina chekka

Cloves
Lavangaalu

Coriander
Dhaniyaala podi (powder)
Kothimeera (leaves)

Cumin
Jeelakarra

Mustard seeds
Aavaalu

Fenugreek seeds
Menthulu

Curry leaves
Karivepaaku

Mint
Pudhina

Turmeric
Pasupu

Saffron
Kumkuma puvvu

Drinks

Water
Neellu

Tip: We call any water as neellu in Telugu. But not all neellu (water) is potable. If you want to ask for potable water, you should say 'manchi neellu (literal: good water)'.

Fun fact: Water is plural in Telugu unlike English. You say "Water **is** coming" in English but "Neellu vasthunna**yi**" in Telugu which literally means "Water are coming".

Juice
Rasam

Beer
Beer

Wine
Wine

Coffee
Coffee

Tea
Tea

Milk
Paalu

Buttermilk
Majjiga

Yoghurt
Perugu

Fruits & Nuts

Tip: Ripe fruits are called pandu/pandlu. Unripe fruits are called kaaya/kaayalu. However, there are some exceptions, for example a coconut is always called as kobbari kaaya, be it ripe or unripe. A simple rule of thumb that can work most of the times is: most of the green fruits can be called as kaaya, and others as pandu.

Fruits
Pandlu

Apple
Apple (colloquial)
Seema regu pandu (traditional)

Banana
Arati pandu (ripe)
Arati kaaya (unripe)

Pear
Pear (colloquial)
Peri pandu (traditional)

Coconut
Kobbari kaya

Orange
Kamala pandu

Lemon/Lime
Nimmakaya

Watermelon
Puchakaaya

Grapes
Draaksha

Mango
Maamidi pandu

Papaya
Boppaya

Almond
Baadampappu

Cashew nut
Jeedipappu

Peanut
Verusenagapappu

Pistachio
Pista pappu

Tip: *All the dry fruits/pulses words in Telugu are suffixed by pappu.*

Vegetables

Vegetable
Kooragaaya

Carrot
Carrot

Murshroom
Puttagodugu

Corn
Mokkajonna

Spinach
Paalakoora

Peas
Pachi battanilu

Cucumber
Keera dhosakaaya

Green chilli
Pachi mirapakaya

Onion
Ullipaaya

Potato
Aloogadda

Garlic
Velluli

Ginger
Allam

Tomato
Tamata

Cabbage
Cabbage

Cauliflower
Gobi puvvu

Eggplant
Vankaya (including mini eggplants that we find in India)

Tip: All green leafy vegetables are considered as aakukuura in Telugu.

Radish
Mullangi

Taste

How is the food
Aaharam/Bhojanam ela undhi

It is delicious
Ruchi ga undhi

It is cold
Challa ga undhi

It is hot (temperature)
Vedi ga undhi

It is hot (spicy)
Kaaram ga undhi

It is sweet
Teeyaga undhi

It is sour
Pulla ga undhi

It is salty
Uppa ga undhi

It is bitter
Vagaru ga undhi

In the kitchen

Kitchen
Vanta gadi/vantillu

Wash
Kadagadam

Cut
Koyyadam

Peel
Chekku teeyadam (remove top layer)

Mix
Kalipadam

Grind
Rubbadam

Fry
Vepudu

Steam
Udakapettadam

Stir
Kalupu

Pan
Pan

Stove
Stove (colloquial)
Poyyi (traditional)

Fridge
Fridge

At the restaurant

May I have a glass of water?
Oka glass manchi neellu isthara?

A table for two people please
Idhariki oka table undha?

Is there a local specialty?
Local special emaina undha?

Can I look at the menu please?
Menu ni chuudagalana?

Is it vegetarian?
Idi shaakaharama?

Is it non-vegetarian?
Idi maamsaharama?

I will take ...
Nenu ... tiskuntanu

I would like a tea
Naaku oka tea kavali

Can you recommend a good restaurant?
Oka manchi restuarant cheppagalara?

Can I have the bill?
Bill ivvagalara?

Chapter 7: Entertainment

Restaurant
Restaurant

Bar
Bar
Mandhu shop

Fun Fact: Medicine is called as "Mandhu" in Telugu and Bar is also called as "Mandhu shop" which literally means "Medical shop". So please do not get misled when you hear "Mandhu shop".

Holidays
Selavalu (Traditional)
Holidays (colloquial)

Travel
Prayanam

Theater
Theater

Cinema/Movie
Cinema (colloquial)
Chithram (traditional)

Let's go for a movie
Cinema ki veldam

Let's watch TV
TV chudham

I am ready to go
Nenu ready (colloquial)
Nenu tayaaru (traditionl)

Where shall we meet?
Manam ekkada kaludham?

Are you free tomorrow evening?
Repu meeru kali aa?

What do you want to do?
Meeku em cheyalani undhi?

I would like to see that movie
Naaku aa cinema chudalani undhi

What is your favorite movie?
Mee favourite cinema enti?
Meeku istamaina cinema enti?

Have you watched that movie?
Meeru aa cinema chusara?

I would like to go to the restaurant
Nenu restaurant ki vellali anukuntunna

I would like to listen to music
Naaku music vinalani undhi

Do you want to play sport?
Meeku aadalani unda?

Who won the game?
Aata evaru gelicharu?

Who got defeated?
Evaru odipoyaru?

I would like to go badminton
Naaku badminton ki vellalani undhi

Tip: Luckily, all sports/games names are english names (except for games that are local to country/state).

Let's go for a walk
Nadudham padha

What did you do yesterday?
Ninna meeru em chesaru?

I had fun
Nenu saradaga gadipanu

My dream is to go to ...
... vellalani na korika

What do you think?
Meerem anukuntunnaru?

It is a good idea
Idi manchi idea (colloquial)
Idi manchi alochana (traditional)

I agree
Nenu angeekaristhanu

I am not sure
Naaku kachitamga telidu

Let me think about it
Deeni gurinchi nannu alochinchanivvu

Count me in
Nannu kuda kalupuko

Chapter 8: Help and emergency

Help!
Sahaayam!

It is an emergency
Idi athyavasara paristhithi

I need...
Naaku ... kavali

I would like...
Nenu ... anukuntunnanu

I need a doctor
Naaku doctor kavali

Are you ok?
Meeru ela unnaru?

Are you afraid?
Bhayam ga unda?

Call an ambulance
Ambulance in pilavandi

Call the police
Police ni pilavandi

Watch out/Careful!
Jagratha/chuskondi!

Stop!
Aapandi!

I had a car accident
Naaku car accident aindi

Can I help you?
Nenu meeku emaina sahayam cheyagalana?

I am sick
Nenu anarogyam ga unnanu

Leave me alone
Nannu vantariga vadileyandi

Don't touch me
Nannu muttukovadhu

Stop following me
Nannu anusarinchadam aapandi

Police!
Police! (colloquial)
Rakshaka bhatulu! (traditional)

Thief
Donga

Can I use your phone?
Nenu me phone vaadukovacha?

Run!
Parigethandi!

Hurry!
Thvaraga!

Slow down!
Nemmadiga!

What happened?
Emaindi?

When did that happened?
Adi eppudu jarigindi?

Don't worry
Chinthinchakandi

Fire!
Mantalu!

Chapter 9: Body

Body
Shareeram

Head
Thala

Hair
Juttu

Eyes
Kallu

Ear
Chevi

Nose
Mukku

Mouth
Noru

Tooth
Pannu

Tongue
Naaluka

Throat
Gonthu

Neck
Meda

Chest
Chaathi

Heart
Gunde

Back
Veepu

Belly
Potta

Arm/Hand
Cheyyi

Finger
Velu

Leg
Kaalu

Knee
Mokalu

Foot
Paadham

Chapter 10: Health and hospital

Hospital
Hospital (colloquial)
Aasupatri (traditional)

I need a doctor
Naaku doctor kavali

I am not feeling well
Naaku ontlo bagoledhu

Take this medicine
Ee mandhu tisukondi

Are you allergic to anything?
Meeku emaina allergy unnaya?
Meeku emaina padava?

I am allergic to...
Nenu ... ki allergic
Naaku ... padadhu

Bleed
Raktha sravam

I am bleeding
Naaku raktham karuthundhi (colloquial)
Naaku raktha sravam ga undhi (traditional)

Pass out
Kallu tiragadam

Pain
Noppi

Where does it hurt?
Ekkada noppi ga undhi?

It is paining here
Ikkada noppi ga undhi

I have a headache
Naaku thala noppi undhi

I hurt my...
Naaku ... daggara dhebba thagilindi

I feel like vomiting
Naaku vaanthi ayyela undhi

I have headache
Naaku thalanoppi ga undhi

My leg is paining
Na kaalu noppi ga undhi

I am bleeding
Naaku raktham kaaruthundhi (colloquial)
Naaku raktha sraavam authundhi (traditional)

I fell
Nenu padipoyanu

I need pain killer
Naaku pain killer kavali (colloquial)
Naaku noppi billa kavali (traditional)

I need cold medicine
Naaku jaubu tablets kavali (colloquial)
Naaku jalubu billa kavali (traditional)

I got the flu
Naaku jalubu chesindi

I have a cramp
Naaku... pattesindi

I have a cough
Naaku daggu ga undhi

I have fever
Naaku jvaram ga undhi

I have difficulties breathing
Naaku uupiri pichukodaniki kastam ga undhi

My heart is paining
Naaku gunde noppi ga undhi

Get well soon
Tvarga kolukondi

Chapter 11: Time

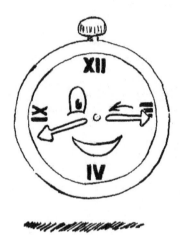

Yesterday
Ninna

Today
Ivalla/Ee roju

Tomorrow
Repu

Second
Second (colloquial)
Kshanam (traditional)

Minute
Nimusham

Hour
Ganta

Day
Roju

Week
Vaaram

Month
Nela

Year
Samvathsaram

Morning
Podhunna/Udayam

Afternoon
Madhyannum

Evening
Saayanthram

Night
Raathri

What day it today?
Ee roju ea vaaram?
Ee roju ea roju?

What time is it?
Time entha?

At what time?
Ea time lo?

Before
Mundara

Now
Ippudu

Late
Aalasyam

Last week
Kindati vaaram

This week
Ee vaaram

Next week
Pai vaaram (colloquial)
Taruvatha vaaram (traditional)

Once a week
Vaaraniki okasari

Everyday
Prathiroju

Always
Prathisari

Never
Eppudu (same word is also used to question *when*)

Not yet
Inka ledhu

Day after tomorrow
Ellundhi

Day before yesterday
Monna

Next time
Vache saari

As soon as possible
Veelainantha tvaraga

We are late
Manam aalasyam ayyam

Wait a moment
Okasari aagandi

Calendar
Panchangam

Note: Panchangam is authentic to Telugu and is based on Telugu year/months/days. Unlike English calendar which is a solar calendar, Telugu panchangam is a lunar calendar. That is the reason why most of the Indian festivals are not celebrated on the same day every year. You can find some people celebrating birthday twice in India, once based on the solar calendar and once based on the lunar calendar.

Days of the week

Monday
Somavaram

Tuesday
Mangalavaram

Wednesday
Budhavaram

Thursday
Guruvaram

Friday
Shukravaram

Saturday
Shanivaram

Sunday
Aadivaram

Note: *Month names are the same as in English except for panchangam but these are not used in everyday life.*

Chapter 12: Family and relationships

Friendship
Sneham

Love
Prema

Friend
Mithrudu/Snehithudu

Family
Kutumbam

Relationship
Sambandham

Elder
Pedha

Younger
Chinna

You are nice
Meeru manchi vyakthi

I trust you
Nenu mimmalni nammuthanu

I do not trust you
Nenu mimmalni nammanu

Are you married?
Meeku pelli ainda? (casual)
Meeru vivahithula? (formal)

I am married
Naaku pelli aindi (colloquial)
Nenu vivahithudni (traditional)

I am engaged
Naaku nischithardham aindi

Do you have children?
Meeku pillalu unnara?

I have two children
Naaku idharu pillalu unnaru

Household
Gruha

Are you coming home?
Meeru intiki vasthunnara?

Go to sleep
Padukondi
Paduko

Can you prepare dinner?
Meeru dinner/bhojanam prepare cheyagalara?

Family members

Mother/Mom
Thalli/Amma

Father/Dad
Thandri/Naanna

Elder brother
Anna/Annayya

Younger brother
Thammudu

Elder Sister
Akka

Younger sister
Chelli

Parents
Thalli thandrulu

Children
Pillalu

Son
Koduku

Daughter
Kuuthuru

Aunt
Atthayya/Pinni/Pedhamma

Uncle
Maamayya/Babai/Pedhananna

Note: Uncle/Aunt is one of the complex relations in Telugu. Please refer to Appendix D to see how this works.

Cousin
Cousin

Note: There is no specific word for cousin in Telugu. Please refer to Appendix D to see how to call cousins in Telugu.

Grand father
Thaathayya/Thaatha

Grand mother
Naanamma (paternal grand mother)
Ammamma (maternal grand mother)

Niece
Menakodalu

Nephew
Menalludu

Wife
Bhaarya

Husband
Bhartha

Mother in law
Athagaru/Athayya

Fater in law
Mamagaru/Mamayya

Brother in law
Bava/Bavagaru (sister's husband)
Bavamaridi/Maridi (husband's/wife's brother)

Sister in law
Vadina

Chapter 13: On the phone

Hello, who is it?
Hello, evaru meeru?
Hello, meerevaru (meeru+evaru)?

This is ... speaking
Nenu ... ni matladuthunnanu

I would like to speak to ... please
Nenu ... tho matladalanukuntunna

Is the President there?
President garu unnara? (casual form)
President garu unnara andi? (formal form)

Note: Earlier you learnt that andi is added to a verb to make it more formal. Here is another new word to be added when you are speaking about someone with respect: you can add "garu" after their name. This is almost like using "sir" in English to speak to someone honourable. Except that in Telugu you will use it more often while talking to/about any elder.

One moment please
Okka kshanam (one second)
Okka nimisham (one minute)

He is not here
Athanu/Aayana ikkada leru
Aayana leru

He will call you back
Aayana malli call chestharu

Can I take a message?
Nenu message tiskogalana?

Could you leave a message?
Meeru emana message ivvlanakuntunnara?

I will call back later
Nenu malli call chesthanu

The phone is ringing
Phone ring authundhi (casual)

I cannot hear you
Naaku vinipinchatledhu

Can you speak louder?
Meeru gattiga matladagalara?

Chapter 14: Emotions and feelings

How are you feeling?
Meeku ela undhi ippudu?

I feel good
Nenu bagunnanu

I am happy
Nenu santhosham ga unnanu

I am sad
Nenu vicharam ga unnanu

I am feeling tired
Nenu alisipoyanu
Naaku alasataga undhi

I am nervous
Naaku gabara ga undhi

I am worried
Naaku kalatha ga undhi

I am angry
Naaku kopam ga undhi

I am bored
Naaku bore kodthundhi (casual)
Naaku em thochatledhu (neutral)

I do not care
Nenu pattinchukonu

I am feeling hot
Naaku vedi ga undhi

I am feeling cold
Naaku challa ga undhi

Are you feeling comfortable?
Meeru sukham ga unnara?

Chapter 15: Animals

Animal(s)
Janthuvu(lu)

Insect
Purugu

What is your favorite animal?
Meeku istamaina janthuvu edi?

My favorite animal is...
Naaku istamaina janthuvu ...

I am scared of dogs
Naaku kukka lu ante bhayam

Do you have any pet home?
Me intlo edaina pempudu janthuvulu unnaya?

Yes, I have three sparrows
Avunu, na daggara muudu pichhukalu unnayi

Cat
Pilli

Dog
Kukka

Bear
Elugubanti

Horse
Gurram

Snake
Paamu

Spider
Saalidu

Frog
Kappa

Elephant
Enugu

Lion
Simham

Tiger
Puli

Leopard
Chirutha puli

Wolf
Thodelu

Rabbit
Kundelu

Cow
Aavu

Rhinoceros
Khadgamrugam

Giraffe
Giraffi

Monkey
Kothi

Mouse
Eluka

Lizard
Balli

Worm
Purugu

Turtle/Tortoise
Thaabelu

Bird
Pakshi

Parrot
Chiluka

Peacock
Nemali

Squirrel
Udutha

Fish
Chepa

Shark
Sorachepa

Whale
Thimingalam

Dolphin
Dolphin

Chapter 16: Weather

How is the weather?
Vaathavaranam ela undhi?

What is the weather forecast?
Vaathavarana suuchana ela undhi?

What will be the weather tomorrow?
Repu vaathavaranam ela untundhi?

Tomorrow it will be sunny
Repu enda ga untundhi

The weather is nice
Vaathavaranam bagundhi

It is sunny
Enda ga undhi

It is cloudy
Mabbu ga undhi

It is raining
Varsham kurusthundhi
Varsham padthundhi

It is hot
Vedi ga undhi

It is cold
Challa ga undhi

It is snowing
Manchu kurusthundhi
Manchi padthundhi

It is windy
Eeduru gali ga undhi

Thunderstorm
Urumu

There is a risk of storm
Tuphanu vache pramadam undhi

There is a risk of flood
Varadalu vache pramadam undhi

There is a risk of showers
Vaana pade pramadam undhi

It hails
Vadagallu pade pramadam undhi

Hailstone
Vadagallu

Chapter 17: Sports

Do you play any sport?
Meeru emana sports adathara? (colloquial)
Meeru emana kreedalu adathara? (traditional)

I play...
Nenu ... adathanu

Did you see the last soccer match?
Meeru chivari football aatanu chusara?

Who won the game?
Aatalo evaru gelicharu?

Yes, it was exiting
Aunu, adi nishkramisthundhi

... is a good player
... manchi aatagadu

What is your favorite team?
Mesku istamaina team edi?

Do you watch sports on the television?
Meeru sports TV lo chusthara? (colloquial)
Meeru aata ni TV lo chusthara? (traditional)

Do you play well?
Meeru baga adathara?

Tournament
Tournament

Indoor
Indoor

Outdoor
Outdoor

Swimming pool
Swimming pool (colloquial)
Eetha kolanu (traditional)

Swim
Eetha

Sports hall
Kreeda sthalam

Fitness club
Gym (colloquial)
Vyaayamashaala (traditional)

Chapter 18: Signals

Entrance
Pravesham

Exit
Nishkramana

Forbidden
Nishedham

Toilets
Marugudhodlu

Open
Terichi undhi

Closed
Muusi undhi

Information
Samaacharam

No smoking
Dhuuamapaanam nishedham

Caution
Hecharika

Telephone
Telephone
STD booth (a public place where you can make paid calls is called STD booth in India)

Police
Police (colloquial)
Rakshakabhatulu (traditional)

Chapter 19: Authority

I must talk to a policeman
Nenu police tho thappakunda matladali

I want to file a complaint
Nenu oka complaint ivvali

Please review your statement
Me statement sari chusukondi

I got robbed
Nenu dongilimpabaddanu
Na meeda dongathanam jarigindi

I lost my wallet
Na purse poindi

Your visa expired
Me visa expire aipoindi

It is forbidden to …
… nishidham

You cannot do that
Meeru adi cheyyakudadhu

Please follow me
Nannu anusarinchandi

There is a misunderstanding
Meeru apaardham cheskuntunnaru

I have not done anything wrong
Nenu elanti thappu cheyyaledhu

Am I under arrest?
Nannu arrest chesthunnara?

Do I have to pay a fine?
Nenu jarimaana chellinchala?

I want to talk to my embassy
Nenu na embassy tho matadali

I need a lawyer
Naaku lawyer kavali

Chapter 20: At work

At work
Pani lo

Office
Office (colloquial)
Kaaryalayam (traditional)

Where is your office?
Me office ekkada?

My office is at...
Na office ... lo

Where do you work?
Meeru ekkada pani chestharu

I work at...
Nenu ... lo pani chesthanu

What is your job?
Me udyogam enti?

Did you receive my e-mail?
Meeku na e-mail vachinda?

This is important
Idi mukyamainadi

I am on leave today
Nenu ivalla leave lo unnanu

I will arrive late today
Nenu ivalla late ga vasthanu

I will leave early today
Nenu ivalla mundara vasthanu

Desk
Balla

Letter
Utharam

Paper
Kaagitham

Book
Pusthakam

Pen
Pen (colloquial)
Kalam (traditional)

Pencil
Pencil

Printer
Printer

Boss
Boss

Employee
Udyogi

Meeting
Samaavesam

I am looking for a job
Nenu udyogam kosam chusthunnanu

I have expérience in …
Naaku … lo anubhavam undhi

I have ten years of experience
Naaku padi ellu anubhavam undhi

Full time job
Full time udyogam (colloquial)
Puurti samayam udyogam (traditional)

Part-time job
Part-time udyogam (colloquial)
Swalpa samayam udyogam (traditional)

Chapter 21: At home

At home
Intlo (Inti + lo)

Room
Gadi

Living room
Hall (colloquial)

Couch/Sofa
Sofa

Dining room
Bhojanala gadi

Table
Balla

Chair
Kurchi

Kitchen
Vanta gadi

Bedroom
Padaka gadi

Bed
Mancham

Wardrobe
Alamara

Bathroom
Bathroom (colloquial)
Snanapu gadi (traditional)

Bath
Snanam

Sink
Sink

Toilets
Toilets (colloquial)
Marugudhodlu (traditional)

Garden
Thota

Tree
Chettu

Flower
Puvvu

Grass
Gadii

Garage
Garage

Chapter 22: Colors

Color
Rangu

What color is this?
Idi ea rangu

White
Thelupu

Yellow
Pasupu

Orange
Naarinja

Intersting fact: The word Naarinja is the origin for english word Orange. It originated from Dravidian language which is the base for many South Indian languages and dialects.

Red
Erupu

Pink
Gulaabi (rose)

Green
Pacha

Purple
Uuda

Blue
Neelam

Brown
Godhuma

Grey
Buudidha (ash)

Black
Nalupu

Light (in color)
Light (colloquial)
Letha rangu (traditional)

Dark
Dark (colloquial)
Muduru rangu (traditional)

Appendix

Telugu alphabets and their sounds

Vowels
a(ʌ), aa(aː), e(i), ee(iː), u(u), uu(uː), ru(ru), ruu(ruː), o(o), oo(oː), au(aw), an(aṅ), aha(aḥ)

Consonants
ka(kʌ), kha(kʰʌ), ga(gʌ), gha(gʰʌ), ṅa(ŋʌ)
cha(tʃʌ), chha(tʃʰʌ), ja(d͡ʒʌ), jha(d͡ʒʰʌ), ña(ɲʌ)
ṭa(ʈʌ), ṭha(ʈʰʌ), ḍa(ɖʌ), ḍha(ɖʰʌ), ṇa(ɳʌ)
ta(tʌ), tha(tʰʌ), da(dʌ), dha(dʰʌ), na(nʌ)
pa(pʌ), pha(pʰʌ), ba(ɓʌ), bha(ɓʰʌ), ma(mʌ)
ya(jʌ), ra(rʌ), la(lʌ), wa(ʋʌ), ḷa(ɭʌ), śa(ɕʌ), ṣa(ʂʌ),
sa(sʌ), ha(ɦʌ), ṛa(ɾʌ), tsa(tsʌ), dza(dzʌ)

Other symbols
aṃ, k

Appendix B

1 – okati
10 – padi
100 – vanda
1000 – veyyi
10000 - padi velu
100000 – laksha
1000000 - padi lakshalu
10000000 – koti
100000000 - padi kotlu
1000000000 - satha koti
10000000000 - veyyi kotlu
100000000000 – nyarbudham
1000000000000 – kharvam
10000000000000 – mahakharvam
100000000000000 – padmam
1000000000000000 – mahapadmam
10000000000000000 - kshoni
100000000000000000 – mahakshoni
1000000000000000000 – sankham
10000000000000000000 – mahasankham
100000000000000000000 – kshiti
1000000000000000000000 – mahakshiti
10000000000000000000000 – kshobham
100000000000000000000000 – mahakshobham
1000000000000000000000000 – nidhi
10000000000000000000000000 – mahanidi
100000000000000000000000000 – paraatham
1000000000000000000000000000 – paraardham

1000000000000000000000000000 – anantham
10000000000000000000000000000 – saagaram
100000000000000000000000000000 – avyayam
1000000000000000000000000000000 – amrutham
10000000000000000000000000000000 – achinthyam
100000000000000000000000000000000 – ameyam
1000000000000000000000000000000000 – bhuri
10000000000000000000000000000000000 – mahabhuri

Appendix C

Savarna deergha sandhi:

When any of the words ending with below letters, encounters the same letter as starting letter of next word, the resulting joining word will replace last letter of first word and first letter of last word with an elongated form (: form) of the encountered word.
A(ʌ), Aa(a:), E(i), Ee(i:), U(u), Uu(u:), Ru(ru), Ruu (ru:)

Below are the possible combinations for this joining:

…a + a… = …aa…
…a + aa… = …aa…
…aa + a… = …aa…
…aa + aa… = …aa…
…e + e… = …ee…
…ee + e… = …ee…
…e + ee… = …ee…
…ee + ee… = …ee…
…u + u… = …uu…
…uu + u… = …uu…
…u + uu… = …uu…
…uu + uu… = …uu…
…ru + ru… = …ruu…
…ruu + ru… = …ruu…
…ru + ruu… = …ruu…
…ruu + ruu… = …ruu…

Example:
Raam**a** + **Aa**layam = Raam**aa**layam

Guna Sandhi:

When A(ʌ) encounters E(i) or Ee(i:), U(u) or Uu(u:), Ru(ru) or Ruu (ru:) the last letter of first word and first letter of second word will be replaced by Ea(e:), Oo(o:), Ar(ʌr) respectively.

...a + e... = ...ea...
...a + ee... = ...ea...
...a + u... = ...oo...
...a + uu... = ...oo...
...a + ru... = ...ar...
...a + ruu... = ...ar...

Example:
Deva + Indrudu = Deveandrudu

Vrudhi Sandhi:

When A(ʌ) encounters Ea(e:) or Ai(aj), last letter of first word and first letter of second word will be replaced by Ai(aj). Also, when A(ʌ) encounters Oo (o:) or Au (aw), last letter of first word and first letter of second word will be replaced by Au (aw).

...a + ea... = ...ai...
...a + ai... = ...ai...
...a + oo... = ...au...
...a + au... = ...au...

Example:
Entha + aindi = enthaindi

Yanadesha Sandhi

When E(i), U(u), Ru(ru) encounters not the same vowel letters (meaning anything other than E(i), U(u), Ru(ru)), last letter of first word and first letter of second word will be replaced by ya (jʌ), wa (ʊʌ), ra (rʌ).

…e + a… = …ya…
…u + a… = …wa…
…ru + a… = …ra…
…e + u… = …ya…
etc…

Example:
Ath**i** + **a**ntha = ath**ya**ntha

Anunasika Sandhi

When ka(kʌ), cha(tʃʌ), ta(ṭʌ), tha(tʌ), pa(pʌ) encounters any of ña(ɲʌ), ṅa(ŋʌ), ṇa(ɳʌ), na(nʌ), ma(mʌ), last letter of first word and first letter of second word will be replaced by ña(ɲʌ), ṅa(ŋʌ), ṇa(ɳʌ), na(nʌ), ma(mʌ) respectively.

…ka + ña… = … ña…
…ka + ṅa… = …ṅa…
…cha + ṅa… = …ṅa…
…ta + ṇa… = …ṇa…
…tha + na… = …na…
…+pa + ma… = …ma…
etc…

Example:
Jaga**th** + **ma**atha = Jagan**ma**tha

Jasthva Sandhi
When ka(kʌ), cha(tʃʌ), ta(t̪ʌ), tha(t̪ʌ), pa(pʌ) encounters any of
1) Vowels
2) Ga(gʌ), gha(gʰʌ), ja(d͡ʒʌ), jha(d͡ʒʰʌ), ḍa(ḍʌ), ḍha(ḍʰʌ), da(d̪ʌ), dha(d̪ʰʌ), ba(ɓʌ), bha(ɓʰʌ)
3) Ha(ɦʌ), Ya(jʌ), wa(ʋʌ), ra(rʌ)
Last letter of first word and first letter of second word will be replaced by ga(gʌ), ja(d͡ʒʌ), ḍa(ḍʌ), da(d̪ʌ), ba(ɓʌ) respectively.

Example:
Jaga**th** + **A**mba = Jaga**dha**mba

Visarga Sandhi
When aha(aḥ) encounters any of
1) Short vowels (not elongated vowels) like A(ʌ), E(i), U(u), Ru(ru), ea(e), O(o)
2) Ga(gʌ), gha(gʰʌ), ña(ɲʌ), ja(d͡ʒʌ), jha(d͡ʒʰʌ), ṅa(ŋʌ), ḍa(ḍʌ), ḍha(ḍʰʌ), ṇa(ɳʌ), da(d̪ʌ), dha(d̪ʰʌ), na(nʌ), ba(ɓʌ), bha(ɓʰʌ), ma(mʌ)
3) Ha(ɦʌ), Ya(jʌ), wa(ʋʌ), ra(rʌ), la(lʌ)
Last letter of first word and first letter of second word will be replaced by Oo (o:)

Example:
Thap**aha** + **Va**namu = Thap**oo**vanamu
There are other alternatives also for this joining but this is the major one.

Akaara Sandhi
When a word ending with consonant sound encounters a word starting with vowel sound, it can result in word joining with different behaviours

Example:
Raa**ma** + **A**yya = Raamayya
This joining is a bit conflicting with Savarna deergha sandhi, the difference is whenever we have Sanskrit orginated words in joinings, it has to be joined based on savarna deergha sandhi (since it is a Sanskrit originated joining). Similarly if the words being joined are Telugu words, then it has to be joined using akaara sandhi.

Ikaara Sandhi
When word ending with e(i) encounters any of Emi, Adi, Avi, Ivi, Edi, Evi, Ki, Mari, Ku, last letter of first word and first letter of second word will be replaced by a new sound.

Example:
Em**i** + **Em**i = Emeami

Ukaara Sandhi
When word ending with U(u) encounters word starting vowel sound, resulting word will not have U(u) in it.

Example:
Nuvv**u** + **e**varu = Nuvvevaru

Dwiruktha takara Sandhi

When word ending with Kuru, Chiru, kadu, nidu, nadu sounds encounter vowel, resulting word will have Tt sound in it.

Example:
Chiru + **e**luka = Chi**tt**eluka

Amreditha Sandhi

When word ending with vowel sound encounters amreditham (if a word is appearing twice as adjacent to each other, second instance of word is called amreditham)

Example:
Ett**a** + **e**tta = Ett**e**tta

Gasadadhavadesha Sandhi

When a second person pronoun encounters ka(kʌ), cha(tʃʌ), ta(tʌ), tha(tʌ), pa(pʌ), resulting joining word will have ga(gʌ), sa(sʌ), ḍa(ḍʌ), da(dʌ), wa(ʊʌ) respectively

Example:
Vaa**du** + **ch**ache = vaadu**s**ache

Pumpvadesha Sandhi

When a verb encounters word starting with mu, resulting word will have pu or pum sound instead of mu sound

Example:
Sarasa**mu** + **ma**ata = sarasa**pu**maata

Saraladesha Sandhi

When 'nu' encounters word starting ka(kʌ), cha(tʃʌ), ta(ʈʌ), tha(tʌ), pa(pʌ), resulting joining word will have ga(gʌ), ja(d͡ʒʌ), ḍa(ɖʌ), da(dʌ), ba(bʌ) respectively.

Example:
Puuche**nu** + **k**aluva = puuchen**ga**luva

These are some of the majot word joinings. They are a few more joinings also but above are most frequently used.

Appendix D

Father
Naanna

Mother
Amma

Brother (elder)
Anna/Annayya

Brother (younger)
Thammudu

Sister (elder)
Akka

Sister (younger)
Chelli

Grandfather
Thaathayya (thaatha as casual)

Grandmother (maternal)
Ammamma

Grandmother (paternal)
Naanamma

Great grandfather
Mutthaatha

Great grandmother
Thaathamma

Husband
Bhartha

Wife
Bhaarya

Aunt (Mother's younger sister)
Chinnamma/Pinni

Aunt (Mother's elder sister)
Pedhamma

Aunt (Father's younger sister)
Attha/Atthayya

Aunt (Father's elder sister)
Attha/Atthayya/Menatha

Uncle (Mother's younger brother)
Maama/Maamayya

Uncle (Mother's elder brother)
Maama/Maamayya/Menamaama

Uncle (Father's younger brother)
Chinnanaanna/Babai

Uncle (Father's elder brother)
Pedhanaanna

Cousin (Mother's sister's son)
Thammudu (if he is younger than you) - Anna/Annayya (if he is older than you)

Cousin (Father's sister's daughter)
Chelli (if she is younger than you) - Akka (if she is elder than you)

Cousin (Mother's brother's son)
Baava (if he is elder than you) - Maridi (if he is younger than you)

Cousin (Mother's brother's daughter)
Vadina (if she is elder than you) - Maradhalu (if she is younger than you)

Brother in law
bava/bavagaru (if he is elder than you) - Bavamaridi (if he is younger than you)

Sister in law
Vadina

Printed in Great Britain
by Amazon